To Give Is to Receive* is the law of Love. Under this law, when we give our Love away to others we gain, and what we give we simultaneously receive. The law of Love is based on abundance; we are completely filled with Love all the time, and our supply is always full and running over. When we give our Love unconditionally to others with no expectations of return, the Love within us extends, expands and joins. So by giving our Love away, we increase the Love within us and everyone gains.

—Gerald G. Jampolsky, M.D.

*From *A Course in Miracles*

LOVE
IS LETTING
GO OF FEAR

Gerald G. Jampolsky, M.D.

Foreword by
Hugh Prather

Illustrated by
Jack O. Keeler

BANTAM BOOKS

TORONTO • NEW YORK • LONDON • SYDNEY • AUCKLAND

*This low-priced Bantam Book
has been completely reset in a type face
designed for easy reading, and was printed
from new plates. It contains the complete
text of the original hard-cover edition.*
NOT ONE WORD HAS BEEN OMITTED.

LOVE IS LETTING GO OF FEAR

*A Bantam Book / published by arrangement with
Celestial Arts*

PRINTING HISTORY

*Celestial Arts edition published October 1979
6 printings through October 1980*

Bantam edition / June 1981

2nd printing . . . . July 1981	6th printing . . . . December 1982
3rd printing . . . . October 1981	7th printing . . . . July 1983
4th printing . . . . December 1981	8th printing . . . . March 1984
5th printing . . . . July 1982	9th printing . . . . August 1984

10th printing . . . . June 1985

*All rights reserved.
Copyright © 1970 by Gerald G. Jampolsky and Jack O. Keeler.
Cover art copyright © 1981 by Bantam Books, Inc.
This book may not be reproduced in whole or in part, by
mimeograph or any other means, without permission.
For information address: Celestial Arts,
Box 7327, Berkeley, CA 94707.*

ISBN 0-553-24518-X

Published simultaneously in the United States and Canada

Bantam Books are published by Bantam Books, Inc. Its trademark, consisting of the
words "Bantam Books" and the portrayal of a rooster, is Registered in U.S. Patent
and Trademark Office and in other countries. Marca Registrada. Bantam Books,
Inc., 666 Fifth Avenue, New York, New York 10103.

PRINTED IN THE UNITED STATES OF AMERICA

O   19   18   17   16   15   14   13   12   11   10

To the children of the universe
Who, by the essence
of their being, Love
Bring light to a darkened world
And lead us to
the Kingdom of Heaven

This book is dedicated to Helen and Bill, who have been both teachers and friends to me. It was because of their joint willingness that *A Course in Miracles* came into being, a work which provides the foundation for this book.

G.G.J.

ACKNOWLEDGMENTS

I wish to express my deep and loving gratitude to Dr. William Thetford for his continued support and encouragement, for the many hours he contributed in modifying and adding content to this book, as well as for his collaboration with me in a previous publication* quoted extensively in *Love Is Letting Go Of Fear.*

In addition, I wish to give my warm thanks to Jules Finegold, Hugh Prather and Mary Abney for their loving assistance in editing.

The twelve lesson titles in this book are quotations from *A Course in Miracles,* copyrighted by the Foundation for Inner Peace, and reprinted here with permission of the publisher. I am especially indebted to Judy and Bob Skutch for both their loving support and for their permission to quote this material.

*To Give Is To Receive: Mini Course For Healing Relationships And Bringing About Peace of Mind, by Gerald G. Jampolsky, M.D., published 1979 by MINI COURSE, P.O. Box 1012, Tiburon, CA 94920.

CONTENTS

Author's Note   1
Foreword   5
Introduction   11

Part I

Preparation for Personal Transformation   15

Part II

Ingredients of Personal Transformation   31

Part III

Lessons for Personal Transformation   45

Lesson 1 /   All that I Give I Give to Myself   49

Lesson 2 /   Forgiveness is the Key to Happiness   63

Lesson 3 /   I Am Never Upset for the Reason I Think   69

Lesson 4 /   I Am Determined to See Things Differently   75

Lesson 5 /   I Can Escape from the World I See
by Giving Up Attack Thoughts   83

Lesson 6 /   I Am Not the Victim of the
World I See   89

Lesson 7 /   Today I Will Judge Nothing that
Occurs   95

Lesson 8 /   This Instant is the Only Time
There Is   103

Lesson 9 /   The Past Is Over—It Can Touch
Me Not   109

Lesson 10 /   I Could See Peace Instead of This   115

Lesson 11 /   I Can Elect to Change All Thoughts
that Hurt   121

Lesson 12 /   I Am Responsible for What I See   127

Epilogue   131

AUTHOR'S NOTE

We teach what we want to learn, and I want to learn to experience inner peace.

In 1975, the outside world saw me as a successful psychiatrist who appeared to have everything he wanted. But my inner world was chaotic, empty, unhappy and hypocritical. My twenty-year marriage had recently ended in a painful divorce. I had become a heavy drinker and had developed chronic, disabling back pain as a means of handling guilt.

It was at this time that I came across some writings entitled *A Course in Miracles.** The *Course* could be described as a form of spiritual psychotherapy that is self-taught. I was perhaps more surprised than anyone when I became involved in a thought system that uses words like *God* and *Love.* I had thought that I would be the last person to be interested in such writings. I had been extremely judgmental toward people who pursued a spiritual pathway; I saw them as fearful and I believed they were not using their intellect properly.

A Course in Miracles, published by the Foundation for Inner Peace, P.O. Box 635, Tiburon, CA 94920

1

When I first began studying the *Course*, I had an experience that was surprising but was also very comforting. I heard an inner voice, or possibly it would be more accurate to say an impression of a voice, which said to me, "Physician, heal thyself: this is your way home."

I found the *Course* essential in my struggle for personal transformation. It helped me recognize that I really did have a choice of experiencing peace or conflict, and that this choice is always between accepting truth or illusion. The underlying truth for all of us is that the essence of our being is Love.

The *Course* states there are only two emotions, love and fear. The first is our natural inheritance, and the other our mind manufactures. The *Course* suggests that we can learn to let go of fear by practicing forgiveness and seeing everyone, including ourselves, as blameless and guiltless. By applying the concepts of the *Course* to both my professional and personal life, I began to experience periods of peace that I had never dreamed possible.

I would like to add that I still get depressed and at times feel guilty, irritable and angry. These moods now last for only brief periods, whereas they used to last for what seemed eternity. I used to feel that I was a victim of the world I saw. When things would go wrong, I would blame the world or those in it for my misery and feel justified in my anger. Today, I know I am *not* a victim of the world I see, and therefore tend to take responsibility for whatever I perceive and for the emotions I experience.

We are all teachers of each other. I have written this book because I believe that in teaching what I want to learn, inner peace, I can become more consistent in achieving it for myself. This approach is not for people who want gurus, since it views everyone equally as both a teacher and a student.

As each of us moves towards the single goal of achieving peace of mind for ourselves, we can also experience the joining of our minds that results from the removal of the blocks to our awareness of Love's presence.

Together, therefore, let us demonstrate in our own lives this statement from *A Course in Miracles:*

Teach only Love for that is what you are.

Jerry Jampolsky
Tiburon, California
May 1, 1979

Love is the way I walk in gratitude.

FOREWORD

I have had many opportunities to watch Jerry in circumstances that could be described as stressful: in the middle of the night, waiting for a teenage girl under our care who had lost her way into one of Chicago's roughest districts; catching meals, naps, planes at odd hours as we traveled across country giving talks; playing tennis at 6:30 in the morning (does that one count?); closed in a room for hours at a stretch with two other people, reaching agreement on almost every word to be included in a book-length manuscript; lost, late for an appointment, retracing our route on California back roads; watching him work with a terminally ill boy in a small and very crowded room, trying to show the boy (and succeeding) how to release himself from pain.

I tell you this so you will know what is behind the following statement: Jerry Jampolsky lives what he teaches. I know that this book comes from the precise center of his heart. Nothing stated here is in the least degree high-flown or impractical. I have seen him live every line of it for as long as I have known him.

My work, in addition to writing books, is with Crisis

5

Intervention. Before that I was a guidance counselor, a school teacher, and a practitioner of spiritual healing (and a few other things less relevant here). One principle circles like a band of light through the activities I have observed in which one person attempts to be of genuine help to another. And I now know, after having seen Jerry's work with victims of accidents and disease, this principle applies whether the one needing help is terminally ill, has brain damage, or is comatose and unable to put his bitter need into words. That principle is: I can be of no real help to another unless I see that the two of us are in this together, that all of our differences are superficial and meaningless, and that only the countless ways we are alike has any importance at all.

I cannot sit down with a father who abuses his child and think, "You bastard, you beat your child; I don't beat mine," and be of any use to that man. If, however, I look honestly at the content of his anger and not the way he expresses it, I will recognize it as my own. All anger felt is expressed in some form, and anger which takes an indirect and devious form is not superior to that which is expressed directly. Recognizing this, I can join with him and turn to that spiritual core that unites us from within, and together we can seek its direction.

The old model of how to be of help to another was based on inequality. I had something "wrong" with me: I was a discipline problem in school, or an alcoholic, or suicidal, or I had a catastrophic illness, or a cold. I was different from you, and it didn't matter what the form that difference took, because in all cases I came to you because I thought you knew more or had skills I lacked.

You then focused your expertise on my problem, and in so doing removed it from the context of my life. It was no longer my problem. I had handed the responsibility for it over to you, and you then told me what to think and do.

If that model had been all there was to our attempts to help each other, I believe little of value would ever have been accomplished. But we have always known its deficiencies, at least intuitively, and this recognition, however vague, allowed for something else. *Love Is Letting Go Of Fear* is about that something else. It is practical because it is *not* new. It is, however, a departure as presented in this book because here it is laid out in as pure a form as possible. As such, it makes this book radical.

Now possibly it could be helpful to some readers if I were to state in my own words my perception of the Jampolsky approach to life. Jerry would say that his is the *Course in Miracles* approach, and I would agree, being a student of those books myself, and yet I add this qualification: Everyone has his unique way of stating the Truth as he sees it, and that uniqueness is important, because there will be only certain people you and I will touch in this lifetime, and for those encounters, honesty will be the container of all the gifts we will give and receive.

Since these will be my words, they may sound more religious than Jerry's, but if you forgive me that difference, I will promise to try to stay within the gentle spirit that is his.

We have been given everything we need to be happy now. To look directly at this instant is to be at peace.

This means we have no interest in how Love will provide for us in the future. And we are unconcerned with what we said or did in the past, or whether someone we think mistreated us will get what he deserves. To be fully content within this moment is a state of mind so powerful in its ability to heal and extend peace that it cannot be even hinted at in words. Anxiety—the only alternative to trusting what is happening—is a state of immobilization caused by our focusing on what we believe cannot be changed: on what is over, or on what has not occurred.

A man called me about two months ago and said he had lost his job, his wife had divorced him, and the woman across the hall in the apartment building where he now lived wouldn't sleep with him. But this latter problem would be alleviated shortly because he was being forced to give up his apartment, and there were no more places to rent. *"A Course in Miracles,"* he said, "does not work."

As we talked, he thought back to the day he had lost his job, and compared the fantasies he had that day about what would happen to what in fact had happened. Although he hadn't been given all he could have imagined wanting, he was provided with everything he truly needed. He agreed that when he looked at it honestly, his moment-by-moment situation had not been unhappy, only his *interpretation* of it had made him feel bad. And this interpretation had to be *remembered*. He had to recall his definition of himself as a fired man. He also found that when he looked closely at what happened following his divorce, love had not been taken from him. It had remained in a form he could understand and appreciate. There were now many others in his life who clearly loved him.

Love itself remains constant; only the particular body from whom we sometimes come to expect it may change. The *Course's* promise that the plan will remain gentle had not been broken. Nor could it possibly be interfered with in the future by a landlord, any more than it had been in the past by an employer. Nothing can interfere with the promise of comfort except our interpretation, and that will always interfere because it will cause us to look dishonestly at where we are and what surrounds us.

This instant we have everything we need, and within this instant we have everything. We can therefore trust what happens because there will never be a time when it will not be now. We are loved. But this Love cannot be seen if we are focusing our minds on everything except what is at hand. Love does not exist in a time of our imagining, and it cannot prove itself trustworthy within our cringing fantasies. We must be willing to rest within its gentle arms, and not concern ourselves with how they got there or why they would choose to remain.

I will close with this lovely story told to me by a friend.

A man who had finished his life went before God. And God reviewed his life and showed him the many lessons he had learned. When He had finished, God said, "My child, is there anything you wish to ask?" And the man said, "While You were showing me my life, I noticed that when the times were pleasant there were two sets of footprints, and I knew You walked beside me. But when times were difficult there was only one set of footprints. Why, Father, did You desert me during the difficult times?" And God said, "You misinterpret, my son. It is true that when the times were pleasant I walked beside you and pointed out the way. But when the times were difficult, I carried you."

Hugh Prather
Santa Fe, New Mexico
June 23, 1979

INTRODUCTION

My friend, Hugh Prather, has written, "There must be another way to go through life besides being pulled through it kicking and screaming."

I believe that there *is* another way of going through life. It requires our willingness to change our goal.

There is an increasing recognition among people everywhere that we are destroying ourselves and the world in which we live. We do not seem to be able to change the world, to change other people, or to change ourselves. Many of us, myself included, have felt the futility of trying to rid ourselves of frustration, conflict, pain and illness, while still holding on to our old belief systems.

Today there is a rapidly expanding search for a better way of going through life that is producing a new awareness and a change of consciousness. It is like a spiritual flood that is about to cleanse the earth. This transformation of consciousness is prompting us to look inward, and as we explore our inner spaces we recognize the harmony and at-one-ment that has always been there.

As we look inward, we also become aware of an inner intuitive voice which provides a reliable source for guidance. When the physical senses are hushed, and we begin to listen to that inner voice and surrender to it, we notice that moments of true healing and growth occur. In this silence, where the conflict of personalities has ceased to interest us, we can experience the joy of peace in our lives.

Although we want to experience peace, most of us are still seeking something else that we never find. We are still trying to control and predict and therefore we feel isolated, disconnected, separate, alone, fragmented, unloved and unlovable. We never seem to get enough of what we think we want, and our satisfactions are highly transitory. Even with those people who are close to us we often have love hate relationships. These are relationships in which we feel a need to get something from someone else; when the need is fulfilled, we *love* them and when it is not fulfilled, we *hate* them. Many of us are finding that, even after obtaining all the things we thought we wanted in terms of job, home, family, money, there is still an emptiness inside. Mother Teresa of Calcutta, India, calls this phenomenon *spiritual deprivation*.

Throughout the world there is a growing recognition of the need to feel fulfillment within, rather than to rely on the external symbols of success. When we have a desire to *get* something from another person or the world and we are not successful, the result is stress expressed in the form of frustration, depression, perceptions of pain, illness and death. Most of us seriously want to get rid of the pain, the illness, and frustrations, but we still want to maintain our old self-concept. Perhaps that is why we are going in circles, because we rigidly hold on to our old belief system.

The world we see that seems so insane is the result of a belief system that is not working. To perceive the world differently, we must be willing to change our belief system, let the past slip away, expand our sense of *now*, and dissolve the fear in our minds. This changed perception leads to the recognition that we are not separate, but have always been joined.

There are many valid pathways that lead to transformation and inner peace. This small book is written as a primer for those of us who are motivated to experience a personal transformation towards a life of giving and Love, and away from a life of getting and fear. In brief, this is a book about self-fulfillment through giving. The words and drawings present practical applications of the steps for transformation to everyday situations that all of us face. It is intended to help us remove the blocks to the awareness of Love's presence, our true reality, so that we may experience the miracles of Love in our lives.

As *A Course in Miracles* suggests, we can have a single *goal* of peace of mind and a single *function* of practicing forgiveness, and our fulfillment can come from listening to the voice of our inner teacher. In so doing, we can learn to heal our relationships, experience peace of mind, and let go of fear.

My present happiness is all I see.

PART I

PREPARATION FOR PERSONAL TRANSFORMATION

All fear is past and only Love is here.

What is Real?

Most of us are confused about what is real. Even though we sense there is something more, we attempt to settle for a reality based exclusively on feedback from our physical senses. To reinforce this "reality," we look to what our culture defines as normal, healthy and therefore real.

Yet where does Love fit into this scheme of things? Wouldn't our lives be more meaningful if we looked to what has no beginning and no ending as our reality? Only Love fits this definition of the eternal. Everything else is transitory and therefore meaningless.

Fear always distorts our perception and confuses us as to what is going on. Love is the total absence of fear. Love asks no questions. Its natural state is one of extension and expansion, not comparison and measurement. Love, then, is really everything that is of value, and fear can offer us nothing because it *is* nothing.

Although Love is always what we really want, we are often afraid of Love without consciously knowing it, and so we may act both blind and deaf to Love's presence. Yet, as we help ourselves and each other let go of fear, we begin to experience a personal transformation.

We start to see beyond our old reality as defined by the physical senses, and we enter a state of clarity in which we discover that all minds are joined, that we share a common Self, and that inner peace and Love are in fact all that are real.

With Love as our only reality, health and wholeness can be viewed as inner peace, and healing can be seen as letting go of fear.

Love, then, is letting go of fear.

Replaying the Past

We all manufacture our own dust and static which serve only to interfere with seeing, hearing and experiencing Love within ourselves and others. This self-imposed interference keeps us stuck in an old belief system that we use repeatedly, even though it doesn't get us what we want.

The mind can be thought of as containing reels and reels of motion picture film about our past experiences. These images are superimposed not only on each other but also on the lens through which we experience the present. Consequently, we are never really seeing or hearing it as it is; we are just seeing fragments of the present through the tons of distorted old memories that we layer over it.

If we are willing, we can with increasing effectiveness use active imagination to wipe away everything from those old reels except Love. This requires letting go of our past attachments to guilt and fear.

Prediction versus Peace

Sometimes we put more value in predicting and controlling than in having peace of mind. At times, it feels more important for us to predict that we are going to be miserable the next moment, and then find pleasure in being right, than to have true happiness in the present moment. This can be looked upon as an insane way of trying to protect ourselves. It produces a short circuit that confuses pleasure with pain.

We often believe that the fears of the past can successfully predict the fears of the future. The results of this type of thinking are that we spend most of our time worrying about both the past and future, creating a vicious circle of fear, which leaves little room for Love and joy in the present.

Choice for Reality

We can choose our own reality. Because our will is free, we can choose to see and experience the truth. We can experience the truth of our reality as Love. To do this, we must, each instant, refuse to be limited by the fearful past and future and by the questionable "realities" we have adopted from our culture. We can choose to experience this instant as the only time there is, and live in a reality of *now*.

Because our minds have no boundaries, they are actually joined. In fact, our minds have only the limitations we place on them. For example, when we see value in making a fearful past "real," we limit our minds to using it as our reality. As a result, our minds can only look fearfully at all that is to come, and cannot pause for an instant to enjoy the present in peace. When we use words such as *can't* and *impossible*, we have imposed the limits of a fearful past on ourselves.

21

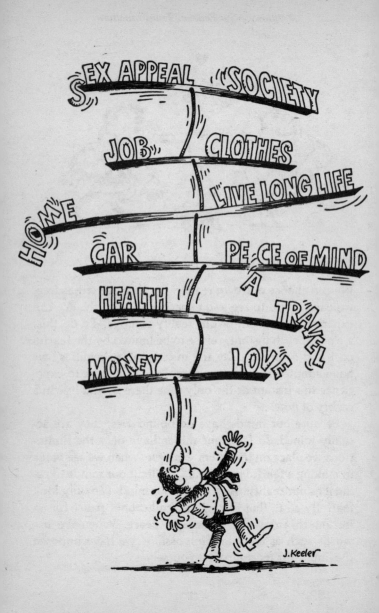

Singleness of Goal

Peace of mind as our single goal is the most potent motivating force we can have. To have inner peace we need to be consistent in having peace of mind as our single goal. Instead of having a single goal, we are all tempted to try to juggle multiple goals. Juggling can only serve to deflect our focus and increase our conflict. We can achieve consistency in keeping this single goal in mind by reminding ourselves of the singleness of purpose we would have if we suddenly found ourselves drowning in the ocean. We would, in that situation, put all of our attention into the single goal of staying afloat and breathing for survival.

Peace of Mind through Forgiveness

With peace of mind as our single goal, forgiveness becomes our single function. Forgiveness is the vehicle used for correcting our misperceptions and for helping us let go of fear. Simply stated, to forgive is to let go.

Our first step in mind retraining is to establish peace of mind as our single goal. This means thinking of ourselves first in terms of self-fullness, not selfishness. The second step is forgiveness.

Many of us become frustrated when we make the mistake of trying to love others as the first step. In light of our past distorted values and experiences, some people simply seem unlovable; because of our faulty perception of their behavior it is difficult to love them.

When we have peace of mind as a single goal, we can then take the second step, forgiveness, and choose to see others as extending Love, or being fearful and calling for help in the form of Love. With this new perception, it becomes easier to give both total Love and acceptance to the other person and therefore to experience inner peace at the same time.

Other people do not have to change for us to experience peace of mind.

Mind as Split

It may be useful to think of the mind as the film, the camera, and everything else involved in movie production. What we experience is really our state of mind projected outward upon a screen called "the world." This world and those in it actually become the mirror of our thoughts and fantasies. What our mind projects becomes our perception, which limits our vision as long as we hold to it.

Our mind functions as if it were split; part of it acts as if it were directed by our egos, and part by Love. Most of the time, our mind pays attention to this pseudo-director that we call our ego, which is simply another name for fear.

The ego directs only movies of war and conflict, although through disguises it makes them appear as if they were the realization of our romantic fantasies. It actually directs only movies that project the illusion that we are all separate from each other. Our true director, Love, does not project illusions; it only extends the truth. Love directs movies that unite and join.

Our mind is actually the director, producer, scriptwriter, film editor, cast, projectionist, audience and critic. Our mind, being limitless, has the capacity of changing the movie and everything about it at any time. Our mind has the power of making all decisions.

The ego part of our mind acts like a curtain of fear and guilt which blocks out Love. We can learn to direct our mind to open the curtain and reveal the light of Love that has always been there and remains our true reality.

When we choose only Love as the director of our mind,

we can experience the power and the miracle of Love.

Themes to Live By

In making practical application of the material covered in this book to everyday situations, it will be helpful to keep the following underlying themes in mind:

1. Peace of mind is our single goal.

2. Forgiveness is our single function, and the way to achieve our goal of peace of mind.

3. Through forgiveness, we can learn not to judge others and to see everyone, including ourselves, as guiltless.

4. We can let go of fear when we stop judging and stop projecting the past into the future, and live only in the now.

5. We can learn to accept direction from our inner, intuitive voice, which is our guide to knowing.

6. After our inner voice gives us direction, it will also provide the means for accomplishing whatever is necessary.

7. In following one's inner guidance, it is frequently necessary to make a commitment to a specific goal even when the means for achieving it are not immediately apparent. This is a reversal of the customary logic of the world, and can be thought of as "putting the cart before the horse."

8. We do have a choice in determining what we perceive and the feelings we experience.

9. Through retraining of the mind we can learn to use positive active imagination. Positive active imagination enables us to develop positive, loving motion pictures in our minds.

**This day I choose to spend
in perfect peace.**

PART II

INGREDIENTS OF PERSONAL TRANSFORMATION

I see all things as I would have them be.

Belief Systems and Reality

We are what we believe. Our belief system is based on our past experience which is constantly being relived in the present, with an anticipation of the future being like the past. Our present perceptions are so colored by the past that we are unable to see the immediate happenings in our lives without distortions and limitations. With willingness, we can reexamine who we think we are in order to achieve a new and deeper sense of our real identity.

We Are All Limitless

To experience this sense of total freedom, it is important for us to detach ourselves from past-future preoccupations and choose to live in the *now*. To be free also means not being confined to the reality that seems limited by our physical senses. To be free allows us to participate in the Love we share with everyone. We cannot be free until we discipline and retrain our minds.

While all of us want Love, many of us seem unable to experience it. Our guilty fears from the past block our ability to give and receive Love in the present. Fear and Love can never be experienced at the same time. It is always our choice as to which of these emotions we want. By choosing Love more consistently than fear, we can change the nature and quality of our relationships.

Attack and Defense

When we perceive another person as attacking us we usually feel defensive, and find a way, directly or indirectly, to attack back. Attacking always stems from fear and guilt. No one attacks unless he first feels threatened and believes that through attack he can demonstrate his own strength, at the expense of another's vulnerability. Attack is really a defense and, as with all defenses which are designed to keep guilt and fear from our awareness, attack actually preserves the problem. Most of us cling to the belief that attacking can really get us something we want. We seem to forget that attacking and defending do not bring us inner peace.

In order to experience peace instead of conflict, it is necessary to shift our perception. Instead of seeing others as attacking us, we can see them as fearful. We are always expressing either Love or fear. Fear is really a call for help, and therefore a request for Love. It is apparent, then, that to experience peace we must recognize that we do have a choice in determining what we perceive.

Many of our attempts to correct others, even when we believe we are offering constructive criticism, are really attempts to attack them by demonstrating their wrongness and our rightness. It may be helpful to examine our motivations. Are we teaching Love or are we demonstrating attack?

If others do not change in accordance with our expectations, we are likely to regard them as guilty, and thus reinforce our own belief in guilt. Peace of mind comes from not wanting to change others, but by simply accepting them as they are. True acceptance is always without demands and expectations.

Forgiveness

Inner peace can be reached only when we practice forgiveness. Forgiveness is the letting go of the past, and is therefore the means for correcting our misperceptions.

Our misperceptions can only be undone *now*, and can be accomplished only through letting go whatever we think other people have done to us, or whatever we think we have done to them. Through this process of selective forgetting, we become free to embrace a present without the need to reenact our past.

Through true forgiveness we can stop the endless recycling of guilt and look upon ourselves and others with Love. Forgiveness releases all thoughts that seem to separate us from each other. Without the belief in separation, we can accept our own healing and extend healing Love to all those around us. Healing results from the thought of unity.

As inner peace is recognized as our single goal, forgiveness becomes our single function. When we accept both our goal and our function, we find that our inner, intuitive voice becomes our only guide to fulfillment. We are released as we release others from the prison of our distorted and illusory perceptions, and join with them in the unity of Love.

Getting and Giving

It is important to remember that we all have everything we need now, and that the essence of our being is Love. If we think we need to get something from another, we will love that person when we get what we think we want, and we will hate that person when we do not. We frequently have love/hate relationships in which we find ourselves trading conditional love. The getting motivation leads to conflict and distress and is associated only with linear time. Giving means extending one's Love with no conditions, no expectations and no boundaries. Peace of mind occurs, therefore, when we put all our attention into giving and have no desire to get anything from, or to change, another person. The giving motivation leads to a sense of inner peace and joy that is unrelated to time.

Retraining the Mind

To aid in retraining your mind, remember to ask yourself the following questions in all circumstances, private or interpersonal:

1. Do I Choose To Experience *Peace Of Mind* Or Do I Choose To Experience *Conflict?*

2. Do I Choose To Experience *Love* or *Fear?*

3. Do I Choose To Be A *Love Finder* Or A *Fault Finder?*

4. Do I Choose To Be A *Love Giver* Or A *Love Seeker?*

5. Is This Communication (Verbal Or Non-Verbal) Loving To The Other Person And Is It Loving To Me?

Many of our thoughts, statements and actions are not loving. If we want peace of mind, it is essential that our communications with others bring about a sense of joining. To have inner peace and to experience Love, we must be consistent in what we think, say and do.

WORDS
THAT KEEP
US IN THE
PAST

J. Keeler

Words to Eliminate

Another process for retraining the mind has to do with recognizing the impact of the words we use. The words in the list that follows are commonly used in the messages we give to ourselves and others. The use of these words continues to keep the guilty past and fearful future active in our minds. As a result, our feeling of conflict can only be reinforced. The more we recognize that using these words interferes with our inner peace, the easier it will be to practice eliminating them from our thoughts and expressions. You may find it helpful to carry an imaginary disposal bag in your mind; every time you use one of these words, visualize yourself putting the word into the disposal bag and then burying it.

It is important always to be gentle with yourself. If you find yourself continuing to use any of these words, merely regard that as a mistake to be corrected and choose not to feel guilty about making a mistake.

Here are the words:

impossible

can't

try

limitation

if only

but

however

difficult

ought to

should

doubt

any words that place you or
anyone else in a category

any words that tend to measure or
evaluate you or other people

any words that tend to judge or
condemn you or someone else

Conclusion

This book provides guidelines for letting go of fear and bringing about inner peace. Its practical applications can help shift our perceptions so that we no longer feel separate, fearful and in conflict, but rather experience joining, Love and peace. Inner peace is experienced as we learn to forgive the world and everyone in it, and thereby see everyone, including ourselves, as blameless.

Each instant of our lives can be regarded as a present opportunity for a new awakening or rebirth, free from the irrelevant intrusion of memories from the past and anticipations of the future. In the freedom of this present moment, we can extend our natural loving nature.

When we find ourselves irritated, depressed, angry or ill, we can be sure we have chosen the wrong goal and are responding to fear. When we are not experiencing joy we have forgotten to make peace of mind our single goal, and have become concerned about getting rather than giving.

By consistently choosing Love rather than fear, we can experience a personal transformation which enables us to be more naturally loving to ourselves and others. In this way we can begin to recognize and experience the Love and joy that unites us.

Review

1. One of the main purposes of time is to enable us to choose what we want to experience. *Do we want to experience peace or do we want to experience conflict?*

2. All minds are joined and are one.

3. What we perceive through our physical senses presents us with a limited and distorted view of reality.

4. We really cannot change the external world nor can we change other people. We *can* change how we perceive the world, how we perceive others, and how we perceive ourselves.

5. There are only two emotions; one is Love and the other is fear. Love is our true reality. Fear is something our mind has made up, and is therefore unreal.

6. What we experience is our state of mind projected outward. If our state of mind is one of well-being, Love and peace, that is what we will project and therefore experience. If our state of mind is one filled with doubt, fear and concern about illness, we will project this state outward, and it will therefore be our experiential reality.

Forgiveness ends all suffering and loss.

PART III

LESSONS FOR PERSONAL TRANSFORMATION

How to Proceed with the Lessons

The specific principles and guidelines found in this book gain personal meaning through the practice of the daily lessons. You may find some of them difficult to accept, or have trouble seeing their relevance to the problems you face in your own life. These uncertainties do not really matter. However, your willingness to practice the lessons without exceptions is important. It is the experience resulting from the practice which will help you approach your goal of greater personal happiness. Remember that willingness does not imply mastery—only a readiness to change one's perception.

Suggestions For Deriving Maximum Benefit From The Lessons:

1. Every day on awakening, relax and use your active imagination. In your mind's eye, put yourself somewhere you would feel comfortable, relaxed and at peace.

2. (Beginning with Lesson 1, do the lessons sequentially, one each day.) Spend a few minutes while you are in this relaxed state repeating the lesson title and

related thoughts several times, allowing them to become part of your being.

3. Each day ask yourself the question, "DO I WANT TO EXPERIENCE *PEACE OF MIND* OR DO I WANT TO EXPERIENCE *CONFLICT*?"

4. Put the lesson title on a card and keep it with you, review it periodically throughout the day and evening, and apply the lesson to everyone and everything without exception.

5. Before retiring, relax again and take a few minutes to review the day's lesson. Ask yourself if you would be willing to have these ideas incorporated in your dreams.

6. When you have completed all of the lessons, your learning will be facilitated if you begin again with the first lesson and repeat the entire series.

7. This form of practice may be maintained until you find that you are thinking about the lessons and applying them consistently without needing to refer to them.

LESSON 1

ALL THAT I GIVE
IS GIVEN
TO MYSELF

All that I Give is Given to Myself

To Give is to Receive is the law of Love. Under this law, when we give our Love away to others we gain, and what we give we simultaneously receive. The law of Love is based on abundance; we are completely filled with Love all the time, and our supply is always full and running over. When we give our Love unconditionally to others with no expectations of return, the Love within us extends, expands and joins. So by giving our Love away we increase the Love within us and everyone gains.

The law of the world, on the other hand, states that what we give away we lose. That is to say, when we give something away, we don't have it anymore and suffer loss.

The world's law is based on the belief in scarcity. It holds that we are never really satisfied. We continue to feel empty as we vainly attempt to get fulfilled by seeking for Love and peace in whatever external forms we have come to think of as desirable.

The problem, of course, is that nothing in our external world will continuously and totally satisfy us. Under the world's law, we continuously search but never find. We frequently think our inner well is empty and that we are in need. We then try to fulfill our imagined needs through other people.

When we expect others to satisfy our desires, and they disappoint us, as they inevitably must, we then experience distress. This distress can take the form of frustration, disappointment, anger, depression or illness. As a result we are likely to feel trapped, limited, rejected or attacked.

When we are feeling unloved and depressed and empty inside, finding someone to give us Love is not really the solution. What is helpful is to Love someone else totally and with no expectations. That Love, then, is simultaneously given to ourselves. The other person doesn't have to change or give us anything.

The world's distorted concept is that you have to get other people's Love before you can feel Love within. The law of Love is different from the world's law. The law of Love is that you *are* Love, and that as you give Love to others you teach yourself what you are.

Today allow yourself to learn and experience the law of Love.

I was mistaken in believing that I could give anyone anything other than what I want for myself. Since I want to experience peace, Love and forgiveness, these are the only gifts I would offer others. It is not charity on my part to offer forgiveness and Love to others in place of attack. Rather, offering Love is the only way I can accept Love for myself.

Example A

The following is a letter from Rita, a friend who came into my life in the fall of 1978. Rita phoned me to ask for help for her teenage daughter Tina, who had leukemia. Tina died in January, 1979.

Rita has given me permission to share this letter which, to me, states with beauty and clarity the essence of today's lesson:

All that I give is given to myself.

February 27

Dear Jerry,

I hope you don't mind being the recipient of these letters, which are my way of expressing my thoughts as they are starting to emerge from some deep, formerly untouched source.

If nothing else, you, as a psychiatrist, know this expression can be therapeutic.

Since I last wrote you, other little threads seem to be weaving into this tapestry of life.

On the 22nd of February, I went to hear Dr. Elizabeth Kubler-Ross speak. Needless to say, it was a real experience. One could hardly come away untouched or unmoved. She touched on some sore spots and some portions of her talk were difficult to endure. But her words, her philosophy, and her work, have made a lasting impression on me, and I feel that what she and you are doing is "what it's all about."

To continue the chronological events which are taking place, this is what happened the next day. I decided to go to work for that one day. During a break, I walked over to a small shopping mall, which I usually frequent. But as I walked over, I noticed a bookstore that hadn't been there previously. I couldn't help wondering from whence it had materialized. I just had to go and look in. I asked how long the shop had been there and I was told, a month. I looked around and noticed some books that had not yet been put on the shelf. One was a book I had heard about and thought I'd like to read one day. I decided to get it. It was Ruth Montgomery's *A World Beyond*. I can't even begin to express the way that book "hit" me. That's a story in itself. But I started to take still another look at my life and ponder where all this was taking me. But, as you said, if the question raised a conflict in me, it wouldn't do me any good. So I didn't dwell on the whys and wherefores. Instead, I re-read your letter and thought about the line where you said that one of the best ways of dealing with what I was going through (mourning) would be to find someone to help. I didn't have to go out and search or even wrack my brain. I knew all along who I was supposed to help.

As briefly as I can, I will tell you the story.

About a year ago, my daughter Tina was beginning to show signs of illness. At the same time, another young woman, twenty years old, who lived two doors away and whom I had known for fifteen years, also came down with a still-undiagnosed illness. The mother and I spoke about our concern and fears about their conditions. Sometime later, when Tina's illness was diagnosed, this lady could not bring herself to talk to me. She never spoke to me the entire time Tina was sick. When Tina died, she came to the Rosary, but she never said a word. A silent look passed between us. She came to the funeral and then was one of the kind neighbors who brought food to the house afterward. In all this time, she never said anything. I knew I was the "reality" of what could happen to her daughter. And so afterward I, too, stayed away so I wouldn't remind her. I always asked other neighbors how she was doing and I always got my information secondhand. Then I thought of you and your letter and words. And I thought "Why not?" I *did* care! And so I went to see her. As soon as she saw me, she came right over to me and we embraced. It was natural! We knew how each other was feeling! It was just beautiful! I felt so good when I left. I wondered why I took so long to walk those few feet to her house. I guess until that point, I just wasn't ready.

But again I say, though you are far away geographically, spiritually you are close. I will not question anything that happens, but accept it and see where it takes me.

Peace to you, Jerry, now and always.

Sincerely,

Rita

Example B

A few years ago I had the good fortune of spending some time in Los Angeles with Mother Teresa, known for her work with the poor and dying in Calcutta, India, and throughout the world. I wanted to meet with her because I knew she demonstrated an almost perfect consistency of living a life of inner peace, and I wanted to learn from her how she did this.

We talked about our mutual work with people who were facing life and death situations. I experienced an inner stillness while in her presence. The power of the Love, the gentility, the peace that emanated from her is difficult to describe. This was something I wanted to experience and demonstrate in myself.

It was the Fourth of July weekend, and I learned she was flying to Mexico City that afternoon. I asked if I could join her because I wanted to continue being in her presence.

She smiled gently and said, "Dr. Jampolsky, I would have no objection about your joining me on the trip to Mexico. But you said you wanted to learn about inner peace. I think you would learn more about inner peace if you would find out how much it costs to fly to Mexico City and back, and give that money to the poor."

I found out the cost of the round trip flight from Los Angeles to Mexico City and gave that amount to the Brothers of Mercy in Los Angeles.

The powerful lesson I learned from Mother Teresa was that I do not have to seek for guidance outside of myself to find out what to do. I learned that the time for giving is always now—not later—and that by giving with no expectations or limits, one has immediate inner peace. I learned in that one instant that all I give is given to myself.

Today I will give to others only the gifts I want to accept for myself.

FORGIVENESS IS THE KEY TO HAPPINESS

Forgiveness is the Key to Happiness

Inner peace can be reached only when we practice forgiveness. Forgiveness is the vehicle for changing our perceptions and letting go of our fears, condemning judgments and grievances.

We need to remind ourselves constantly that Love is the only reality there is. Anything we perceive that does not mirror Love is a misperception. Forgiveness, then, becomes the means for correcting our misperceptions; it allows us to see only the Love in others and ourselves, and nothing else.

Through selective forgetting, through taking off the tinted glasses that superimpose the fearful past upon the present, we can begin to know that the truth of Love is forever present and that by perceiving only Love we can experience happiness. Forgiveness then becomes a process of letting go and overlooking whatever we thought other people may have done to us, or whatever we may think we have done to them.

When we cherish grievances we allow our mind to be fed by fear and we become imprisoned by these distortions. When we see our only function as forgiveness, and are willing to practice it consistently by directing our minds to be forgiving, we will find ourselves released and set free. Forgiveness corrects the misperception that we are separate from each other, and allows us to experience a sense of unity and at-one-ment with each other.

Forgiveness, as defined here, is different from the way most of us have been trained to understand it. Forgiveness does not mean assuming a position of superiority and putting up with or tolerating behavior in another person that we do not like. Forgiveness means correcting our misperception that the other person harmed us.

The unforgiving mind, contrasted with the forgiving mind, is confused, afraid and full of fear. It is certain of the interpretation it places on its perceptions of others. It is certain of the justification of its anger and the correctness of its condemning judgment. The unforgiving mind rigidly sees the past and future as the same and is resistant to change. It does not want the future to be different from the past. The unforgiving mind sees itself as innocent and others as guilty. It thrives on conflict and on being right, and it sees inner peace as its enemy. It perceives everything as separate.

Whenever I see someone else as guilty, I am reinforcing my own sense of guilt and unworthiness. I cannot forgive myself unless I am willing to forgive others. It does not matter what I think anyone has done to me in the past or what I think I may have done. Only through forgiveness can my release from guilt and fear be complete.

Example

The following is a personal vignette that demonstrates some principles about grievances and forgiveness.

One morning my secretary brought in a huge pile of bills. She reminded me that my income was down because of the increasing amount of time I was spending on a non-fee basis. She said there was a man who owed me $500 for services rendered to his daughter the previous year, and reminded me how well and quickly his daughter had responded to working with me. Then she said that she was tired of sending the bill and suggested I send it to a collection agency.

I told her I had never sent a bill to a collection agency, and didn't plan to do that now, but I would give some thought to the matter. As I looked at the unpaid bills I owed, I began to feel what I thought was justified anger, and I felt I had a legitimate grievance. After all, I had done my part, and he and his daughter had benefited from working with me. I knew the father could well afford to pay the fee, and I began to think he was a louse for not paying. I made up my mind to phone him that afternoon.

While meditating on my daily lesson from *A Course in Miracles*, which was "Forgiveness is the key to happiness," a picture of this man who owed me money came across my mind. I heard an inner voice state that I was to let go of the past and my attachment to the money. I was to practice forgiveness and heal my relationship with him.

So I phoned him. I told him about my meditation and my decision to send no more bills. I told him of my past anger and of my determination not to retain it. I said I was calling to heal our relationship, and that the money was no longer an issue. There was a long pause before he said, "Well, if I don't pay your bill, certainly God is not going to."

I said I thought it important to let go of the money issue and the anger I had felt toward him regarding the bill. I told him I was releasing myself from the thought that he had hurt me in any way.

There was another silence, and his voice became warm and loving. He thanked me for phoning and then to my surprise he said he would mail the check next week (which he did).

The next hour I saw a mother of an eleven-year-old girl who had cancer of the spine and was a member of one of our groups at the Center. The mother had been receiving public assistance, but because of many complexities was not able to obtain money through this or other channels. Her car had been repaired and was waiting for her at the garage, but she could not pay the $70 repair bill. Because of the car problem, she had missed essential appointments for her daughter's chemotherapy treatments. My inner voice said, "Give her the $70 since you have just found money that you thought you didn't have." When I did this, I experienced inner peace. I continue to be impressed by how quickly I experience inner peace when I let go of my attachment to the past belief that someone is guilty and someone is innocent.

Today I choose to let go of all my past misperceptions about myself and others. Instead, I will join with everyone and say: I see you and myself only in the light of true forgiveness.

LESSON 3

I AM NEVER UPSET
FOR THE REASON
I THINK

I Am Never Upset for the Reason I Think

Most of us have a belief system based on experiences from the past and on perceptions from the physical senses. Have you considered that what we believe is what we see? Or, as comedian Flip Wilson put it, "What you see is what you get."

Because our physical senses appear to relay information from the outside world to our brain, we may believe that our state of mind is controlled entirely by the feedback we receive. This belief contributes to a sense of ourselves as separate entities who are largely isolated and feel alone in an uncaring and fragmented world. This can leave us with the impression that the world we see causes us to feel upset, depressed, anxious and fearful. Such a belief system presumes that the outside world is the cause and we are the effect.

Let us consider the possibility that this type of thinking is upside down and backwards.

What would happen if we believed that what we see is determined by the thoughts in our mind? Perhaps we could entertain an idea that may at the moment seem unnatural and foreign to us; namely, that our thoughts are the cause and what we see is the effect. It would then make no sense to blame the world or those in it for the miseries and pain we experience, because it would be possible then to consider perception as "a mirror and not a fact."

Consider once again that the mind may be like a motion picture camera, projecting our internal state onto the world. When our mind is filled with upsetting thoughts, we see the world and those in it as upsetting to us. On the other hand, when our mind is peaceful, the world and the people in it appear to us as peaceful. We can choose to awaken in the morning and see a friendly world through glasses that filter out everything except Love.

It may be helpful to question our need to attempt to control the external world. We can, instead, consistently control our inner world by choosing what thoughts we want to have in our mind. Peace of mind begins with our own thoughts and extends outward. It is from our peace of mind (cause) that a peaceful perception of the world arises (effect).

We all have the power to direct our minds to replace the feelings of being upset, depressed and fearful with the feeling of inner peace.

I am tempted to believe that I am upset because of what other people do or because of circumstances and events which seem beyond my control. I may experience being upset as some form of anger, jealousy, resentment or depression. Actually, all of these feelings represent some form of fear that I am experiencing. When I recognize that I always have the choice between being fearful or experiencing Love by extending Love to others, I need no longer be upset for any reason.

Example

For many years I had been bothered by chronic disabling back pain. Through those years I was not able to play tennis, garden, or do many of the things that I liked to do. I was hospitalized several times, and at one point the neurosurgeon wanted to perform surgery on what was called an organic back disease—a degenerative disc. I chose not to have the surgery.

I thought I was upset because of the pain and the distress caused by it. Then one day there seemed to be a small voice inside which said that, even though I had an organic back syndrome, I was causing my own pain. It became clear to me that my back condition became worse when I was under emotional stress, particularly when I was fearful and holding a grievance against someone. I was not upset for the reason I thought.

As I learned to let go of my grievances through the practice of forgiveness, my pain disappeared. I now have no limitations on my activities.

I thought I had been upset because of back pain. I found, however, I was upset because of unhealed personal relationships. I had let myself believe that the body controls the mind, rather than realizing that the mind controls the body. I feel certain that most people who have back problems have the potential to learn to let go of their grievances, their guilt and fears, and through forgiveness of others and themselves experience their own healing.

Throughout the day, whenever you are tempted to be fearful, remind yourself that you can experience Love instead.

LESSON 4

I AM DETERMINED
TO SEE THINGS
DIFFERENTLY

I Am Determined to See Things Differently

The world we see that seems so insane may be the result of a belief system that isn't working. The belief system holds that the fearful past will extend into a fearful future, making the past and the future one. It is our memory of fear and pain that makes us feel so vulnerable. It is this feeling of vulnerability that makes us want to control and predict the future at all costs.

I would like to present a personal example. I was reared in a family where a fearful attitude always seemed to prevail. I bought into a philosophy that said, "The past is awful, the moment is horrendous, and the next moment is going to be worse." And, of course, we were all correct in our predictions since we shared the same assumptions.

Our old belief system assumes that anger occurs because we have been attacked. It also assumes that counterattack is justified in return, and that we are responsible for "protecting" ourselves, but are not responsible for the need to do so.

If we are willing, it is possible to change our belief system. However, to do so we must take a new look at every one of our cherished assumptions and values from

the past. This means letting go of any investment in holding on to fear, anger, guilt or pain. It means letting the past slip away and with it all the fears from the past that we keep extending into the present and future.

"I am determined to see things differently" means that we are truly willing to get rid of the past and future in order to experience *now* as it really is.

Most of my life I have acted as if I were a robot, responding to what other people said or did. Now I recognize that my responses are determined only by the decisions I make. I claim my freedom by exercising the power of my decision to see people and events with Love instead of fear.

Example A

When I was in medical school, a surprising percentage of the class came down with whatever disease was being discussed. It made no difference what the disease was; it could have been hepatitis, schizophrenia or syphilis.

My thing was tuberculosis. When I was an intern in Boston I had to spend one month on the TB service and I was scared to death that I would catch tuberculosis and die. My fantasy plan was to take one deep breath as I went on the ward and not breathe for a month. I was a total wreck at the end of my first day.

That night about 11:30 I received an emergency call. I ran to the ward where a fifty-year-old woman, who not only had tuberculosis but was also an alcoholic with cirrhosis of the liver, had just vomited blood. She was pulseless. I massaged her heart and removed the blood from her throat with a suction machine. The oxygen machine would not work at first and I administered mouth-to-mouth resuscitation. Her pulse came back and she began to breathe. She made it.

After I went back to my intern quarters I saw myself in the mirror and I was a bloody mess. All of a sudden it occurred to me that I had not been fearful at any time during the episode.

That night I learned that when I was totally absorbed in what I might get, I was immobilized with fear and was a help to no one, but when I was totally absorbed in giving, I felt no fear. By letting go of the past, by putting my full attention into giving in the now, I forgot about fear and could see things differently.

Perhaps it is needless to say I immediately lost my fear of tuberculosis. That patient turned out to be a very potent teacher for me.

Our state of mind is our responsibility. Whether we experience peace or conflict is determined by the choice we make in how we see people and situations, whether we see them as worthy of Love or as justifying our fear.

We do not have to act like robots and give others the power to determine whether we will experience Love or fear, happiness or sadness.

Example B

This book emphasizes that a shift in perception can reverse our way of thinking; that it helps when you put the cart in front of the horse.

I am finding that when personal guidance has established the goal (the cart), all I need do is keep that goal firmly in my mind and the means (the horse) will take care of itself. Most of us expend so much energy in trying to find the means that we lose sight of the goal.

Here is a recent example: The children I work with who have catastrophic illnesses recently wrote a book. It looked as if it would take eighteen or more months to get it published through an established publishing house. Although we did not have any money, my guidance was not to wait but to publish the book ourselves, and to have faith that somehow the money would be

provided. (In the past I would never have done anything like this without having the money first. This time, however, I was determined to see things differently.)

I did make a personal commitment to the printer that I would borrow the money from the bank if we were not able to raise the necessary funds. On a Friday at noon, the 5,000 copies of the book, *There is a Rainbow Behind Every Dark Cloud*, were delivered. We had raised less than 10 percent of the money required.

I felt as if I were at the end of a high diving board and someone was about to push me off. However, one hour later we received a phone call from the Executive Director of the Bothin Foundation, stating that they had approved our grant application and we would immediately receive a check paying for the books in full.

Through this experience, I learned that nothing is impossible when we follow our inner guidance, even when its direction may threaten us by reversing our usual logic.

Whenever you feel tempted today to see through the eyes of fear, repeat to yourself with determination:

"I am not a robot; I am free.
I am determined to see things differently."

LESSON 5

I CAN ESCAPE
FROM THE WORLD
I SEE BY
GIVING UP
ATTACK
THOUGHTS

I Can Escape from the World I See by Giving Up Attack Thoughts

Many of us feel at times that we are hopelessly trapped in the world we see. Try as we may, we just can't seem to change the world and escape from its seeming confines.

If we remember that it is our thoughts that make up the world, then we can change them. We change the world we see by changing our thoughts about it. By changing our thoughts, we are actually changing the cause. Then the world we see, the effect, will change automatically.

A changed thought system can reverse cause-and-effect as we have known it. For most of us, this is a very difficult concept to accept, because of our resistance to relinquishing the predictability of our past belief system and to assuming responsibility for our thoughts, feelings and reactions. Since we always look within before looking out, we can perceive attack outside us only when we have first accepted attack as real within.

We forget this premise when we perceive another person as attacking us. We try to hide from our conscious awareness that the attack we perceive as coming from others actually originated in our mind. When we recognize this, we can become aware that our attack thoughts are actually hurting ourselves. We may then choose to replace attack thoughts with Love thoughts in order to stop hurting ourselves. Our higher self-interest brings with it the understanding that the Love we give to others strengthens the Love we have for ourselves.

Once again, it may be worthwhile to remind ourselves that attack thoughts do not bring us peace of mind and justifying our anger doesn't really protect us.

I recognize today that my attack thoughts about others are really directed against myself. When I believe that attacking others brings me something I want, let me remember that I always attack myself first. I do not wish to hurt myself again today.

Example

The Center for Attitudinal Healing has recently received considerable national publicity through television and other media because of our work with children with catastrophic illnesses. We have, because of the thousands of letters received, started a national and international pen pal and telephone network in which children around the world are finding peace by helping each other. This work was producing enormous telephone bills and we were in need of money.

Recently, because I was preoccupied with this problem, I was quieting my mind through meditation, and the thought occurred to me that I was to call the president of Pacific Telephone Company and elicit his financial help. I found this guidance difficult to accept for two reasons. The first was that I felt I had already paid my dues in asking people for money and just did not want to do that anymore. The second reason was that one of my pet hates was the telephone company. My phone was frequently out of order and I often found myself irritated and angry at the telephone company.

However, my inner voice was persistent. I felt that I could not call them while I was still angry. So what I did was to spend the next two weeks practicing forgiveness and letting go of my attack thoughts. To my surprise I was then able to feel a sense of oneness, a joining, and Love between me and the people at the telephone company.

I then tried to phone the company president and, of course, couldn't get through to him. My fantasy was that there were about fifty people protecting him from callers who were angry and wanted to complain. I always got the same message, "The president is busy and can't talk to you now."

After calling him four times, I decided to try only once more. To my surprise, he answered the phone himself. I told him why I wanted to see him and, rather than referring me to their public relations department, he made an appointment with me.

He could not have been more cordial. Almost immediately, a committee from the phone company began to evaluate our Center, and six weeks later we were awarded a grant of $3000.

Now, as far as I am concerned, *that is a miracle!* And in my heart I do not believe that this miracle could ever have happened unless I had let go of my attack thoughts to uncover the Love that was already there.

Throughout the day when you are tempted to hurt yourself through attack thoughts, say with determination:

> I want to experience peace of mind right now.
> I happily let go all attack thoughts and
> choose peace instead.

LESSON 6

I AM NOT
THE VICTIM OF
THE WORLD
I SEE

I Am Not the Victim of the World I See

Have you noticed how often you feel that you are a victim of the world in which you live? Because most of us perceive many aspects of our surroundings as insane, we are tempted to feel helplessly caught in a trap. When we allow ourselves to think we are living in an unfriendly environment where we must fear being hurt or victimized, we can only suffer.

To be consistent in achieving inner peace, we must perceive a world where everyone is innocent.

What happens when we choose to see others as free from guilt? How can we begin to look at them differently? To begin with, we might have to look on everything in the past as irrelevant except the Love we have experienced. We could choose to see the world through the window of Love rather than the window of fear. That would mean we would then selectively choose to see the beauty and the Love in the world, people's strengths rather than their weaknesses.

What I see without is a reflection of what I have first seen within my own mind. I always project onto the

world the thoughts, feelings and attitudes which preoccupy me. I can see the world differently by changing my mind about what I want to see.

Example A

In the past, I thought it was healthy and culturally supported to feel paranoid when walking into a dealership to buy a car. Car salesmen were not to be trusted. To be suspicious of them was as normal as it was wise, and I could have given you selected experiences to prove my case. What I did not realize was that all this approach was doing for me was to eliminate my choices. I found myself with only one attitude, that of fear and suspicion. Peace of mind was impossible.

I was not even aware that the salesman was probably operating from his own set of selected past experiences which "taught" him to be distrustful of customers. He had "learned" that they were disrespectful of him and

had only some form of degradation to offer. By seeing himself as being perceived by his customers as a second-class citizen, all he was accomplishing was to see himself that way.

The car salesman and I had one thing in common—a perception of each other that was totally distorted. And the means by which we had blurred our vision was the same. We had selected only certain aspects from our pasts to form a judgment by which we measured each other in the present.

I am now consulting at a large car agency and I find that my attitudes are changing. Together, we are exploring letting go of our past grievances, and we are putting our efforts into practicing forgiveness.

What would happen if customers and car salesmen saw clearly that the past is irrelevant and could thereby release it, and so become Love finders rather than fault finders, Love givers rather than Love seekers? Perhaps, then, we would all be free to approach each other with the extension of peace as our only motivation. The misperception, "I am the victim of the world I see," could then be changed to, "I am *not* the victim of the world I see."

Example B

Through others hearing of our work at the Center, I was asked to see Joe, a fifteen-year-old boy whose head had been run over twice by a tractor. He was rendered blind, mute and sensationless, and had a bilateral spastic paralysis. He was in a coma for months and the doctors felt even a miracle would not help him.

However, his family never gave up hope for Joe's improvement and tried to live one day at a time, making the utmost of their *now*. As Joe began to regain consciousness, he worked hard and was determined to recover completely. Then, what seemed like a series of miracles began to happen. Joe recovered his speech and began to walk. Throughout this period he spent much time helping others.

When I saw him, Joe's spirits seemed to be up almost all the time. I asked him how he maintained this mood, and he replied, "Oh, I just look at the positive things in everyone—and pay no attention to the negative things, and refuse to believe in the word, 'impossible'."

Joe doesn't often feel sorry for himself. He could feel that the universe had dealt him a horrible blow. However, he chooses peace instead of conflict by deciding to see the world and those in it through the window of Love. *There is a choice.*

To me, Joe is pure Love. He just exudes it. He and his family are powerful teachers of Love for me and many others. He perfectly exemplifies the statement, "I am not the victim of the world I see." Sometimes when I am feeling down I think of Joe. I am then reminded that I, too, can choose not to see myself as a victim of the world I see.

Throughout the day, whenever you are tempted to see yourself as victimized, repeat: Only my loving thoughts are real. It is only these I would have in this situation (specify) or with this person (specify).

TODAY
I WILL JUDGE
NOTHING
THAT OCCURS

Today I Will Judge Nothing that Occurs

Have you ever given yourself the opportunity of going through just one day concentrating on totally accepting everyone and making no judgments? Most of us think we would find that a very difficult task, since it is a rare occurrence to spend a few moments, let alone a whole day, with someone without making a judgment. When we think about it, many of us will be appalled at how often we condemn others and ourselves. We may even feel that it is almost impossible to stop being judgmental. However, all that is really necessary is our willingness to begin practicing being non-judgmental, without expecting instant perfection. The relinquishing of old habits that we do not want comes with repeated and sustained practice.

Most of us manifest a condition which could be called "tunnel vision." We do not see people as a whole. We see just a fragment of a person and our mind often interprets what we see as a fault. Most of us were brought up in a home and school environment where emphasis was placed on constructive criticism, which actually is usually a disguise for faultfinding.

On those occasions when we observe ourselves repeating this same mistake with our spouses, our chil-

dren, our friends, or even someone seen only casually, it may be helpful for us to quiet our minds, observe our thoughts, and become aware that being a faultfinder is totally dependent on our past experiences.

Evaluating and being evaluated by others, a habit from the past, results at worst in fear and at best in conditional love. To experience unconditional Love, we must get rid of the evaluator part of ourself. In place of the evaluator, we need to hear our strong inner voice saying to ourselves and others, "I totally Love and accept you as you are."

As we reinforce our decision to be only Love finders, it becomes easier for us to concentrate on the strengths of others and overlook their weaknesses. It is important that we apply this lesson to everyone, including ourselves. That means that we can also see ourselves in a Loving way.

Not judging others is another way of letting go of fear and experiencing Love. When we learn not to judge others—and totally *accept* them, and not want to *change* them—we can simultaneously learn to accept ourselves.

Everything we think, say or do reacts on us like a boomerang. When we send out judgments in the form of criticism, fury or other attack thoughts, they come back to us. When we refrain from making judgments and send out only Love, it comes back to us.

Today, be willing not to make a condemning judgment against anyone you meet, or even think about. See everyone you meet or think of as either extending Love, or as being fearful and sending out a call for help, which is a request for Love.

Example A

I recently had a powerful learning experience in regard to my attack thoughts. It had been a particularly busy day. I had arranged to have a boy with terminal brain cancer and his mother fly from Connecticut to California. They arrived to be my house guests late in the afternoon. That evening I brought them to the Center. There was a meeting that night with other children who had catastrophic illness. After it was over I took them to my home and returned to the Center to assist in another meeting of adults who had various forms of cancer.

That meeting was to be over at 9:30 p.m. and I was to go to a friend's house to meet some guests from India. When I started to leave the Center, there was a young man of about eighteen years of age waiting to see me. He had a beard, was untidy in appearance, and smelled like he had not had a bath in weeks.

He said he wanted to talk to me. I was tired and anxious to leave and didn't really want to see anyone else who had a problem. He said he had just arrived after hitchhiking from Virginia, that he had seen me on a national television show and felt guided to meet me.

My inner thoughts were quite judgmental. "He must be quite disturbed to come across the country to meet me because he saw me on television." His request to see me seemed like a demand and an attack. I told him I had another appointment that evening and that I could see him the next day if he thought he could wait. Otherwise, I would stay and see him. He said he could wait.

The next day he was not able to be specific about what he wanted except to say there was something in my eyes that made him want to see me. Since neither of us seemed to know why he was there, I suggested that we meditate together and that perhaps we might get an answer.

As we meditated, I was surprised to hear a clear inner voice state, "This man came across the country as a gift to you to tell you he saw perfect Love in your eyes—something that you have difficulty seeing in yourself. Your gift to him is to demonstrate total acceptance to him, something he has never in his life experienced."

I shared with him what I had heard and we put our arms around each other. I was amazed to realize that the awful odor I had smelled only a moment before had totally disappeared. Tears came down both of our faces and a mutual peace and Love was experienced that is difficult to describe.

A healing had taken place for both of us. Attack thoughts had been replaced by Love thoughts. We truly had been teachers and psychotherapists for each other. There didn't seem to be anything more to do or say.

We departed in extreme joy. I had a feeling I would never see him again but that I would never forget the experience and the lesson of forgiveness that he had taught me.

Example B

I think most of us can identify with the man who goes to a fashionable restaurant for dinner, and finds the service simply awful and the waitress brusque, rude and unfriendly. We can also identify with what would seem like justified anger, a reasonable grievance, hostile fantasies and his leaving the waitress no tip.

To have inner peace as our single goal we need to cor-

rect the erroneous belief that justified anger or grievances bring us peace. Anger and attack simply do not
bring peace of mind.

Now let us start this small drama over again. This
time I whisper into the patron's ear, just as he sits down,
that the husband of the waitress died two days ago and
that she has five children at home who are solely dependent on her for their support.

Now, he can see the waitress as fearful, and recognize
that she is giving a call for Love. He can now respond by
seeing her strength and devotion, and he finds he can
overlook (forgive) her behavior. His response now is a
loving, accepting attitude which he demonstrates by
leaving an extra-large tip.

The external form of what is seen by the eyes and ears
is the same in both dramas. However, in the first script,
the events are seen through the window of fear, and in
the second, through the window of Love.

**Today, allow yourself to have the single goal of inner
peace by putting all your attention on the following
thoughts: Today I will view without judgment everything that occurs. All events provide me with another
opportunity to experience Love in place of fear.**

THIS INSTANT IS THE ONLY TIME THERE IS

This Instant is the Only Time There Is

I have often thought that we have much to learn from infants. They have not yet adapted to the concept of linear time with a past, present and future. They relate only to the immediate present, to right *now*. It is my hunch that they do not see the world as fragmented. They feel that they are joined to everything in the world as part of a whole. To me, they represent true innocence, Love, wisdom and forgiveness.

As we become older, we tend to accept the adult values which emphasize projecting past learning into the present and anticipated future. It is difficult for most of us to have even the slightest question about the validity of our past-present-future concepts. We believe that the past will continue to repeat itself in the present and future without the possibility of change. Consequently, we believe we are living in a fearful world where, sooner or later, there will be suffering, frustrations, conflict, depression and illness.

When we hold on to, invest in and become attached to our guilty experiences and grievances from the past, we are tempted to predict a similar future. The future and the past then become one. We feel vulnerable when we believe that the fearful past is real and forget that our only reality is Love, and that Love exists this instant. Feeling vulnerable, we expect that the past will repeat itself. We see what we expect, and what we expect we both invite and seek. Past guilt and fears are thereby continually recycled.

One way of letting go of our "archeological garbage" is to recognize that holding on to it does not bring us what we want. When we see no value in recycling it, we remove the blocks to our being free to forgive and Love completely now. Only in this way can we be truly happy.

"This instant is the only time there is" can become an eternity. The future becomes an extension of a peaceful present that never ceases.

My preoccupation with the past and its projection into the future defeats my aim of present peace. The past is over and the future is yet to be. Peace cannot be found in the past or future, but only in this instant.

I am determined to live today without either past or future fantasies. I will remind myself: This instant is the only time there is.

Example

The following letter is from a nurse named Karol who has become a dear friend. We had previously talked together about how healing (the inner peace that comes from letting go of fear) can take place in an instant.

February 25

Dear Jerry,

Recently I've been in numerous situations where I've talked on and on about unconditional love and the importance of honoring the very essence of one's own being by letting go of fear. I guess we talk most about the very things we are learning.

In a dream, I was sitting face-to-face with a human being—ugly, fearful, deformed and miserable. For a brief instant I wanted to run away. But as I relaxed, coming into myself, I saw the very real connection between us and I loved this connection. As I saw the illusional aspect of the ego interpretation fade away, a bright light emitted the radiance, divinity and innocence nobody had seen before. I embraced this person with a genuine love I'd never experienced. This person received my love, and there was a rejoicing and a communion with a spiritual merging of souls. This person was myself and I was this person; we celebrated our oneness. I knew the real feeling of love, honor and forgiveness. I shall never forget the absolute and complete healing that took place in an instant. I truly understand what you were saying *now*.

> In Truth and Love,
>
> Karol

I wanted to share this beautiful letter with you because gifts are to be shared. I continue to find Karol's letter helpful to me at those times when I become attached to the past and am having trouble forgiving myself and others.

This instant is the only time there is.

THE PAST IS
OVER
IT CAN
TOUCH ME NOT

The Past Is Over—It Can Touch Me Not

When we think we have been hurt by someone in the past, we build up defenses to protect ourselves from being hurt in the future. So the fearful past causes a fearful future, and the past and future become one. We cannot Love when we feel fear. We cannot Love when we feel guilt. When we release the fearful past and forgive everyone, we will experience total Love and a oneness with all.

We seem to consider it "natural" to use our experiences of the past as reference points from which to judge the present. This results in our seeing the present with distorted dark-colored glasses.

Familiarity may not always breed contempt, but it is likely to dull our perceptions of those with whom we have close relationships. If we are to see our spouse, boss or co-workers as they truly are, we must see them now, by recognizing their past and our own have no validity in the present.

To let each second be a new birth experience is to look without condemnation on the present. It results in totally releasing others and ourselves from all the errors of the past. It allows us to breathe in freedom and experience the miracle of Love by sharing this mutual release.

It allows for an instant of healing where Love is ever present, here and now.

It is our investment in wanting to control and predict that keeps us attached to the painful and guilty experience of the past. Guilt and fear, which are allied and which our minds make up, stimulate us to believe in this continuity of time.

If we feel that someone rejected us, criticized us or was unfair to us in the past, we will see that person as attacking us. This reinforces our fear and we attempt to attack back. Releasing the past means not blaming anyone, including ourselves. It means holding no grievances and totally accepting everyone, making no exceptions. It means a willingness to see only the light in others, and not their lamp shade.

Fear and Love, guilt and Love, cannot co-exist. Only if I keep reliving the past in the future am I a slave to time. By forgiving and letting go of the past, I free myself of the painful burdens I have carried into the present. Now I can claim the opportunities for freedom in the present without my past distortions.

Example

In 1975, I conducted a seminar on *A Course in Miracles* a few months after I had become a student of these writings. At the intermission, a couple in their sixties came up to me and said that they were going to visit their thirty-five-year-old son, a chronic schizophrenic, in the state hospital the next day. They asked my advice about how to apply the principles of the *Course* to their visit.

I didn't really know what to say, so I asked my intuitive self for guidance. What came out of my mouth surprised me. The words didn't seem like mine, although they will be familiar to you because they have since become part of me and therefore part of this book. I responded by saying:

"Spend as much time as you can before tomorrow ridding yourself of all the past, painful, guilty, fearful thoughts and experiences you have had with your son. Release yourselves from any guilt you have about your son's condition. Use active imagination and put all your fears, guilts and pain in a garbage can and attach the can to a yellow balloon filled with helium. Print on the balloon, *I forgive my misperceptions.* Then watch the balloon and garbage can disappear into the sky. Pay attention to how much lighter and freer you feel.

"When you go to the hospital and the doctor talks to you about your son's behavior, do not be attached to what he has to say. Look past what your eyes and ears report. Choose to see your son only through the window of Love. Choose to see your son only as light—the light of Love. See the light of Love in your son and the light of your Love as one light. Feel the peaceful bliss

and know that the function of Love is to unite all things unto itself."

A week later I received a beautiful gift, a letter from the parents saying that they had experienced the most peaceful visit with their son they had ever had.

Today I choose to claim my release from past pain and suffering by living only in the immediate present.

114

I COULD SEE PEACE INSTEAD OF THIS

I Could See Peace Instead of This

Most of us go through life with the belief system that our happiness or unhappiness is largely determined by the events in our environment and reactions of other people to us. Frequently we feel that our happiness is dependent on good or bad luck for which we bear little responsibility.

We forget to instruct our minds to change our perceptions of the world and everything in it. We forget that peace of mind is an internal matter and that it is from a peaceful mind that a peaceful perception of the world is experienced.

The temptation to react with anger, depression or excitement exists because of interpretations we make of the external stimuli in our environment. Such interpretations are necessarily based on incomplete perception.

When we dwell on past events or anticipate future happenings, we are living in the realm of fantasy. Whatever is real in our lives can only be experienced now. We block the possibility of fresh and novel experience in our lives when we attempt to relive in the present our memories of episodes from the past, whether painful or pleasurable. We are, therefore, in a continual state of conflict about the actual happenings of the present and are unable to directly experience the opportunities for happiness which are all about us.

Most of the time I see a fragmented world where nothing seems to make much sense. The bits and pieces of my daily experience reflect the chaos I see within. Today, I welcome a new perception of myself and the world.

Example A

My mother is eighty-eight years old. As a fifty-four year old man, I still frequently find myself wanting to please her, and to change the many situations that make her unhappy. When I find my efforts unsuccessful I feel uneasy, and I am then tempted to perceive my mother as demanding and rejecting when she is simply asking for help.

I find that I need to remember that I *am* responsible for the emotions I experience, and that my mother didn't cause my lack of peace—I did.

The lesson, "I could see peace instead of this," reminds me that the choice is between peace or conflict. When consistently practicing this lesson I then can choose to see my mother differently. I can choose to accept my mother without wanting to change her. This perception leads to seeing the Love that exists between us and the recognition that she continues to be a most significant teacher of mine.

Example B

When we are ill, the temptation is to complain, pity ourselves, focus attention on our bodies and feel disabled by our discomfort and pain. In this state, our feelings of anger, irritability and depression only reinforce a generalized sense of helplessness and hopelessness.

We are finding in our work with the children at the Center that through our willingness to help others we can learn to be happy rather than depressed. These children are teaching us that when we are ill or disabled, we can choose to direct our minds away from our bodies and their ailments and focus all of our attention on being truly helpful to others.

The moment we put our attention on helping someone, we cease to perceive ourselves as ill or in pain, and find meaning in the statement, *"To give is to receive."*

Repeat to yourself whenever you feel that your peace is threatened by anything or anyone: I choose to see the unity of peace instead of the fragmentation of fear.

I could see peace instead of this.

I CAN ELECT TO CHANGE ALL THOUGHTS THAT HURT

I Can Elect to Change All Thoughts that Hurt

That free will and choice are inherent attributes of the mind is something most of us tend to forget. We have all had the experience of feeling trapped in a situation where there seemed to be no escape.

Here is a suggestion which may prove helpful under such circumstances. You can use active imagination to find a way out. Picture a wall and let it represent your problem. On this wall paint a door and hang a red exit sign above it. Imagine yourself opening the door, walking through it and shutting it firmly behind you. Your problem is no longer with you, since you have left it behind. Experience your new found freedom by imagining yourself in a place where you have no worries and there is nothing to do other than what you would enjoy. When you are ready to leave your happy retreat, bring with you this newly-found sense of release from past problem solving attempts. In the freshness of your new perception, solutions previously unavailable to you will now occur.

If we perceive things not as problems but rather as opportunities for learning, we can experience a sense of joy and well-being when the lessons are learned. We are never presented with lessons until we are ready to learn them.

In my mind are thoughts that can hurt me or help me. I am constantly choosing the contents of my mind, since no one else can make this choice for me. I can choose to let go of everything but my Loving thoughts.

Example

The following personal vignette may help to illustrate today's lesson. The episode took place in 1951 at Stanford Lane Hospital, which was then located in San Francisco.

The situation was one in which I felt trapped and immobilized by fear. I was feeling emotional pain, and thought I was threatened with potential physical pain. The past was certainly coloring my perception of the present, and I was surely not experiencing inner peace or joy.

I was called at 2 A.M. one Sunday morning to see a patient on the locked psychiatric ward who had suddenly gone berserk. The patient, whom I had not seen before, had been admitted the previous afternoon with a diagnosis of acute schizophrenia. About ten minutes before I saw him, he had removed the wooden molding from around the door. I looked through the small window in the door, and saw a man six feet four inches tall weighing 280 pounds. He was running around the room nude, carrying this large piece of wood with nails sticking out, and talking gibberish. I really didn't know what to do. There were two male nurses, both of whom seemed scarcely five feet tall, who said, "We will be right behind you, Doc." I didn't find that reassuring.

As I continued to look through the window, I began to recognize how scared the patient was, and then it began to trickle into my consciousness how scared I was. All of a sudden it occurred to me that he and I had a common bond that might allow for unity—namely, that we were both scared.

Not knowing what else to do, I yelled through the thick door, "My name is Dr. Jampolsky and I want to come in and help you, but I'm scared. I'm scared that I might get hurt, and I'm scared you might get hurt, and I can't help wondering if you aren't scared, too." With this, he stopped his gibberish, turned around and said, "You're goddamn right, I'm scared."

I continued yelling to him, telling him how scared I was, and he was yelling back how scared he was. In a sense we became therapists to each other. As we talked, our fear disappeared and our voices calmed down. He then allowed me to walk in alone, talk with him and give him some oral medication and leave.

This was a very powerful and important learning experience for me. At first I saw the patient as a potential enemy who was going to hurt me. (My past told me that anyone who seemed disturbed and had a club in his hand was dangerous.) I chose not to use the manipulative device of authority which would have only served the purpose of creating more fear and separation. When I found a common bond in our fearful attitudes and sincerely asked for his help, he joined me. We were then in a position of helping each other. When I saw this patient as my teacher rather than my enemy, he helped me recognize that perhaps we are all equally insane and that it is only the form of our insanity that is different.

I am determined today that all my thoughts be free from fear, guilt or condemnation, whether of myself or others, by repeating: I can elect to change all thoughts that hurt.

I AM
RESPONSIBLE
FOR WHAT I SEE

I Am Responsible for What I See

I choose the feelings I experience, and I decide

upon the goal I would achieve.

And everything that seems to happen to me,

I ask for, and receive as I have asked.

**Teach only Love for that
is what you are.**

EPILOGUE

Let us consistently choose the single goal of peace rather than multiple goals that lead to conflict. Let us continue to practice forgiveness and to see each other and ourselves as blameless. Let us look lovingly upon the present, for it holds only knowledge that is forever true. Let us continue to be involved in a process of personal transformation in which we are only concerned about giving, and not about getting.

Let us recognize that we are united as one Self and illuminate the world with the light of Love that shines through us. Let us awaken to the knowledge that the essence of our being is Love, and, as such, we are the light of the world.

Bantam
On Psychology

☐	25119	**HONORING THE SELF** Nathaniel Branden	$3.95
☐	23767	**HOPE AND HELP FOR YOUR NERVES** Claire Weekes	$3.95
☐	24279	**SIMPLE EFFECTIVE TREATMENT OF AGORAPHOBIA** Claire Weekes	$3.95
☐	23874	**HOW TO BREAK YOUR ADDICTION TO A PERSON** Howard M. Halpern, Ph.D.	$3.95
☐	01419	**IF YOU COULD HEAR WHAT I CANNOT SAY . . .** Nathaniel Branden (A Large Format Book)	$8.95
☐	22576	**PATHFINDERS** Gail Sheehy	$4.50
☐	24754	**PASSAGES: PREDICTABLE CRISES OF ADULT LIFE** Gail Sheehy	$4.95
☐	23399	**THE POWER OF YOUR SUBCONSCIOUS MIND** Dr. J. Murphy	$3.95
☐	34182	**GOODBYE TO GUILT** Gerald Jampolsky, M.D. (A Large Format Book)	$6.95
☐	34139	**TEACH ONLY LOVE** Gerald Jampolsky (A Large Format Book)	$6.95
☐	24518	**LOVE IS LETTING GO OF FEAR** Gerald Jampolsky	$3.50
☐	23818	**PEACE FROM NERVOUS SUFFERING** Claire Weekes	$3.95
☐	24064	**THE BOOK OF HOPE** DeRosis & Pellegrino	$4.50
☐	23449	**THE PSYCHOLOGY OF SELF-ESTEEM: A NEW** Nathaniel Branden	$3.95
☐	25023	**WHAT DO YOU SAY AFTER YOU SAY HELLO?** Eric Berne, M.D.	$4.50
☐	24038	**PSYCHO-CYBERNETICS AND SELF-FULFILLMENT** Maxwell Maltz, M.D.	$3.95
☐	24557	**THE DISOWNED SELF** Nathaniel Branden	$3.95
☐	24411	**CUTTING LOOSE: An Adult Guide for Coming To Terms With Your Parents** Concept of Man's Psychological Nature Howard Halpern	$3.95
☐	25197	**WHEN I SAY NO, I FEEL GUILTY** Manuel Smith	$4.50

We Deliver!
And So Do These Bestsellers.

SPECIAL
MONEY SAVING
OFFER

Now you can have an up-to-date listing of Bantam's hundreds of titles plus take advantage of our unique and exciting bonus book offer. A special offer which gives you the opportunity to purchase a Bantam book for only 50¢. Here's how!

By ordering any five books at the regular price per order, you can also choose any other single book listed (up to a $4.95 value) for just 50¢. Some restrictions do apply, but for further details why not send for Bantam's listing of titles today!

Just send us your name and address plus 50¢ to defray the postage and handling costs.